MW00988815

This document is geared towards providing exact and reliable information in regards to the topic and issue covered. The publication is sold with the idea that the publisher is not required to render accounting, officially permitted, or otherwise, qualified services. If advice is necessary, legal or professional, a practiced individual in the profession should be ordered.

- From a Declaration of Principles which was accepted and approved equally by a Committee of the American Bar Association and a Committee of Publishers and Associations.

The information provided herein is stated to be truthful and consistent, in that any liability, in terms

Table of Contents

Introduction

In our present modern era, oftentimes, cooking is only for a single person. If you are in this category, you know how it feels to go to the trouble of fixing a meal that takes too much effort and time.

This has made single people resort to frozen meals heated in a microwave as answer to the need for a hot and satisfying meal.

Preparing meals can be delightful and a healthy option since the ingredients used are personally chosen and handled by only you. The downside is the big portions you get when you opt out to cook your own food. Leftovers can be simply that left over meal that stays inside the fridge until it's time to chuck it out.

The advent of mug meals has dispensed with all these food problems. Now you can have your cake (literally) and eat it too!

Let me share with you the wonderful, delicious, and exciting mug meal recipes that are perfectly portioned every mealtime. Cooking for yourself has now been elevated to a higher and better level with these scrumptious mug meals for breakfast, lunch, snacks, dinner, and desserts.

Come with me as we travel through the gastronomic delights of mug meals!

Chapter 1 - What are Mug meals?

The hottest trend has happened to cooking with the advent of mug meals. Unless you've been living in a cave, under the rock, or simply not in, mug meals have become the craziest and most wonderful cooking style invented!

There was a time when one-pot meals were the most practical cooking idea for people who wants to prepare their meals in advance. Then somebody cooked up the idea of mug meals with recipes as far ranging as pasta, couscous, omelets, and, yes, cakes! The list of cooking ideas using a single mug goes on and on to fit any craving, time, and place.

Ingredients may vary but the cooking style and tools needed do not. All you need to start your very own mug meals is a mug, a microwave, your choice of ingredients, this recipe book, your creativity, and you're off!

Chapter 2 - Mug dishes to start your day right

It cannot be emphasized enough that breakfast is the most important meal of the day simply because it is the meal to start a new day. Sadly, it is also the meal that people tend to skip most because preparing breakfast can be time-consuming especially when you are in a hurry.

Here are some breakfast mug meal ideas you can prepare in a jiffy and enjoy eating to start your day right:

2-minute Omelet

Ingredients:

2 eggs

2 tablespoons of milk

2 tablespoons of grated cheese

Herbs, pepper, salt, as per preference

Instructions:

- Spray a bit of cooking oil in a 12 oz. cooking dish or microwave-friendly coffee mug
- Beat the eggs and milk in the mug until well-blended
- Zap them in the microwave for 45 seconds with dial turned HIGH
- Stir the eggs and remove from microwave once set
- Top the eggs with herbs, cheese or salt and pepper

Quick mug oatmeal with Apple and Banana

Ingredients:

1 tbsp. of flax seed, ground

1/3 mashed banana

½ chopped apple

1 egg

½ cup of quick cooking oats

¼ tsp of cinnamon

½ cup of milk

2 tsp of honey

Instructions:

- In a microwave-friendly mug, mix together flax, milk, oats, and egg.
- Use a fork to stir them well
- Add to the mixture honey, banana, apple, and cinnamon
- Mix them all well using the same fork
- Turn the microwave on high and cook the mixture for 2-3 minutes
- In between cooking time you can add more milk or butternut if you want
- Fluff the mixture before it's set
- That's it. Enjoy your healthy and delicious breakfast!

A Mug of Blueberry Pancake

A microwave, a microwave-friendly mug, frozen or fresh blueberries and some common ingredients is all it takes to make this delightfully delicious pancake for breakfast! You can also substitute frozen or fresh strawberries or any fruit you want instead of using blueberries.

Ingredients:

1 tablespoon of frozen or fresh blueberries

1 tablespoon of milk

¼ tsp of baking soda

1 egg

3 tbsp. of flour, all purpose

1 tbsp. of vegetable oil

2 tsp of agave or honey maple syrup

Instructions:

- In a microwave-friendly mug, mix all the ingredients minus the frozen or fresh blueberries
- Stir them thoroughly until batter becomes smooth
- Add the frozen or fresh blueberries
- Zap the batter in the microwave for about 1 minute or 1 minute and 15 seconds

- Pancake is cooked when it is firm to the touch
- Drizzle a bit of maple syrup
- Top with a bit of blueberries
- Add more maple syrup and blueberries
- Eat and enjoy!

Quiche Mug

Ingredients:

Chives, freshly chopped or fresh leaves of thyme

Salt

1 egg

½ slice or ham or prosciutto

Dijon mustard

Black pepper, ground per taste

2 tsp of cream cheese

¼ of French bread or a bagel

Instructions:

- With the use of a fork, beat milk and egg in a microwave-friendly mug
- Season with pepper and salt per preference
- Tear pieces of bread into dime size and add to the mixture
- Stir in the cream cheese
- Cut into small pieces the ham or prosciutto

- Stir in the mixture and top with chives or thyme
- Zap in the microwave, which should be turned on high for around 1 minute (60 seconds)
- Top with either chives, mustard or thyme

A Mug of Cinnamon Roll Cake

Ingredients:

For the cake:

1/8 tsp of salt (scant)

2 tbsp. of applesauce

2 ½ tbsp. light-brown sugar, tightly packed

1 tbsp. of vegetable oil

¼ tsp of baking powder

¼ tsp of vanilla extract

1 pinch of nutmeg, ground (optional)

¼ cup and 1 tbsp. of flour, all-purpose

1 tbsp. of buttermilk

¾ tsp of cinnamon

For the frosting:

1 tsp of milk

1 tbsp. of softened Neufchatel Cheese or Cream Cheese

2 tbsp. of powdered sugar

Instructions:

- In a small bowl, combine all the ingredients for the frosting until smooth. Set aside
- In a microwave-friendly mug, use a fork to whisk all the cake ingredients until batter becomes almost smooth
- Set microwave heat to high and nuke the mug for 1 minute
- If cake remains uncooked, zap for another 15 seconds
- Remove the cake and let it cool a bit
- When cake becomes warm, top it with the Cream Cheese frosting
- Breakfast is served!

A Mug of Egg White Omelette

Ingredients:

4 lightly beaten egg whites

2 tbsp. of turkey bacon or ham, fully cooked

2 tbsp. of shredded fresh baby spinach

1 tbsp. of diced green pepper

1 tbsp. of diced red pepper

1 tbsp. of cheddar cheese, reduced-fat

Salt and pepper as per preference

Instructions:

- Spray non-stick cooking spray in a microwave-friendly mug
- Mix all the ingredients in the mug, blending them well
- Turn heat to high on microwave and zap the mixture for 1 minute or 1 ½ minutes until egg has set
- Drizzle with your favorite sauce or eat it as it is
- Time to start your day!

Chapter 3 - Mug Meal Lunch Box

Lunch can be a treat using less cooking and cleaning time with these mouth-watering mug recipes. These recipes can even be cooked using the microwave in your workplace to give you a hearty, hot, and delicious lunch.

A Mug-full of Cheese and Macaroni

More time can be saved if you prepare this meal well ahead of time and microwaving them the next day to give you a hot and filling lunch. You would also be surprised how quick and easy it is to cook pasta using a microwave.

Ingredients:

4 tablespoons of grated cheddar cheese

1 oz. /28g or 1/3 cup of preferred pasta

Salt and pepper to taste

6fl oz. /175ml or ¾ cup of cold water

¼ tsp of corn flour or cornstarch

4 tbsp. of milk

Instructions:

- Use a large mug or bowl that is microwave-friendly. You need a bigger mug so water can't boil over it
- Add water and macaroni in the mug

- Microwave them for about 3 ½ minutes or until pasta is cooked
- Pour off any water from the cooked pasta
- Add grated cheese, milk, and corn starch to the cooked pasta and zap it for 60 seconds more
- Stir the mixture well, adding pepper and salt to season

Tip: Keep a watchful eye on the mug while pasta is being cooked in the microwave so you can stop the process when it overflows and to keep it from becoming overcooked.

A mug of Fried Rice with Egg

Fried rice is a delicious and filling lunch meal which can also be cooked in a mug! This quick and easy recipe will show you how:

Ingredients:

1 cup of cooked rice

1 tiny pinch of purple cabbage

1 tbsp. of low-sodium Soy Sauce

½ tsp of onion powder

½ tsp of sesame oil

2 tbsp. of frozen peas

2 tbsp. of red pepper

1 large egg

½ green onion, sliced

¼ tsp of Five-spice powder

1 tiny pinch of Mung bean sprouts

Instructions:

- Use a larger mug for this recipe. You may also need to cover cling wrap over the mug while microwaving it. Just remember to punch a tiny hole on top of the wrap to prevent scalding when it's time for you to remove it

- Before putting on the cling wrap, top all vegetables on the rice, and microwave it for 1 minute
- While waiting, beat one large egg and add in the five-spice powder, soy sauce, onion powder, and sesame oil
- Remove the mug from the microwave, remove the wrap and pour in the egg mixture, mixing them well
- Put the cling wrap back on the mug and zap it in the microwave for 1 minute and 15 to 30 seconds
- Remove the mug, remove the wrap, and stir the rice
- Let it steam for a minute to steep the flavors and fluff the rice with a fork
- Make yourself comfortable and enjoy your meal

Vegetable Soup cooked in a Mug

Ingredients:

1 egg

1 chopped carrot

Water as per preference

1 stalk of chopped celery

1 tbsp. of any preferred flavor bouillon

Optional: 1 chopped jalapeno peppers

Instructions:

- Using a microwave-friendly mug, put all the ingredients except the egg
- Put a 1" space near the top of the mug
- Water should only be enough to cover the vegetables
- Zap for 3-4 minutes in the microwave, which should be turned high
- Watch that water does not go over the mug
- Break an egg to the mixture, making sure that the yolk is broken open
- Put the mug back in the microwave and zap for another 1-2 minutes or until egg is cooked
- Enjoy your hot and healthy lunch!

Healthy Greek Couscous Salad in a Mug

This healthy salad gives healthy benefits as well as a hearty lunch meal to fill and energize you. The ingredients may be more than what you expect from the usual mug meal recipes, but preparation time is quick and easy. You can prepare the ingredients beforehand and be able to whip up this lunch in no time at all!

Ingredients:

1 tbsp. of feta, crumbled

1/3 cup of couscous, uncooked

¼ cup of cucumber, chopped

Pinch of salt

1 tbsp. of green onion, chopped

1/3 cup of water or chicken broth

1 tbsp. of halved kalamata olives

1 ½ tsp of olive oil

½ medium-sized and chopped Roma Tomato

1 tsp of lemon juice

Instructions:

- Pour water or chicken broth in a microwave-friendly mug and zap it in the microwave for 3 minutes

- Remove the mug, add couscous, and cover for 5 minutes
- With the use of a fork, fluff the couscous
- Add salt, lemon juice, and olive oil, stirring until well-mixed
- Stir in the green onions, cucumber, olives, and tomato
- Top the salad with crumbled feta
- Enjoy the healthy and delicious goodness of your salad!

A Mug of Edamame, Pineapple and Rice

Ingredients:

2 tbsp. of cashews, chopped

1/3 cup of Edamame, frozen and shelled

½ cup of instant brown rice

1 tbsp. of teriyaki sauce

2/3 water

¼ cup of canned pineapple, drained or fresh pineapple, diced

Optional additions of green onion, hot pepper sauce or fresh mint, chopped

Instructions:

- Use a 16-ounce microwave-friendly mug
- Combine water and rice in the mug
- Top with Edamame
- Cover the mug with saucer or small plate
- Turn microwave to high and zap the mug for 5-6 minutes or until little water is left
- Remove, let stand with cover for 1 minute to let water become more absorbed
- After a minute, remove the cover, and add the teriyaki sauce and pineapple.
- Stir until well-mixed
- Zap in the microwave again, this time uncovered for 30-45 seconds

- Let the mug stand for 30 seconds before seasoning with hot sauce if preferred
- Drizzle with cashew nuts
- Time to enjoy your lunch!

Pizza and Egg in a Mug

Ingredients:

½ tsp of low-fat grated topping, Parmesan-style

2 tbsp. of crushed tomatoes from a can

6 slices of chopped turkey pepperoni

1/8 tsp of Italian seasoning

1 wedge creamy light Swiss cheese

1 liquid egg substitute, fat-free

Instructions:

- Combine Italian seasoning and crushed tomatoes in a small bowl
- Spray non-stick to a large microwave-friendly mug, add the egg substitute and zap it in the microwave for 1 minute
- Remove the mug and add the cheese wedge by breaking or crumbling it in the egg mixture

- Return to the microwave and zap it for another 30 seconds
- Remove and add the chopped pepperoni and the mix of tomatoes and seasoning
- Return the mug to the microwave and zap for 30 seconds until mixture is set
- Garnish with grated topping
- Stir

Chapter 4 - Dinner Mug Meals

Dinner can easily be the best meal of the day. Nothing can be more satisfying and stress-relieving than a good hot meal. With the advent of the mug meals, dinner is elevated to a new level of gustatory experience.

Here are some exciting dinner mug meal recipes to waken up your taste buds:

A delicious mug of Ricotta and Spinach Lasagna

Ingredients:

1/3 cup of partly-skimmed mozzarella cheese

2 ½ cups of baby spinach

6 tbsp. of tomato sauce or pasta sauce

½ fresh Lasagna sheet

¼ cup of partly-skimmed ricotta cheese

¼ tsp of salt, Kosher

1/8 tsp of granulated garlic

¼ of medium-sized yellow bell pepper

3 large Basil leaves

Instructions:

- Make a ½ strip cut in a sheet of fresh lasagna. Make another ½ strip cut on the strip

- In a large bowl, place the lasagna sheets and pour hot boiling water on them until covered. Set aside.

- Get the spinach, chop them, and put them in a microwave-friendly bowl. Cover the bowl with cling wrap, making sure to slit a small hole in the middle. Zap it for a minute, remove, and set aside

- While waiting for the spinach to cool down, get the mozzarella and begin grating

- As soon as spinach cools, mix salt, ricotta, granulated garlic, and pepper in it and set aside
- Get a mug, and pour the pasta sauce in it. Get a softened lasagna sheet and put it over the sauce.
- Top the spinach mixture with 2 tbsp. of mozzarella, and another lasagna sheet
- Build it up by alternately topping lasagna sheet, spinach mix, and mozzarella.
- End with a lasagna sheet, with only mozzarella topping it
- Zap them in the microwave for a minute and a half or until mozzarella is all melted. Zap for another 15 seconds if mozzarella is not melted and continue at intervals of 15 seconds until it becomes melted
- Enjoy your dinner!

Salmon in a Mug

Fancy a bit of salmon for dinner? Sure you can with this easy salmon-in-a-mug recipe that might well become an all-time favorite.

Ingredients:

2-3 slices of lemon freshly cut

1 single filet of salmon

1 tbsp. of parsley

2 tbsp. of mayonnaise

Salt and pepper to taste

1-2 tbsp. of sriracha sauce

Instructions:

- You need to use a bigger container/wide-mouth microwave-friendly mug to hold your salmon
- Use cold water to rinse your salmon and pat dry afterwards
- Put the salmon in the container, skin-side down
- Season with pepper and salt as per preference and put aside
- Mix sriracha sauce and mayonnaise in a small bowl
- Spread the mixture generously on the salmon

- Garnish with parsley and slices of lemon
- Wrap the container tightly with cling wrap
- Zap the salmon for 3 and a half minutes or until done
- Use a fork to check the center of the fish to see if it's cooked
- Add another 30-45 seconds cooking time if the fish is still uncooked
- Top with additional slices of lemon and parsley
- Enjoy!

A Mug of Meatball Stew, Italian Style

Ingredients:

Black pepper, ground and salt to taste

1/3 cup of mixed vegetables in a can, drained

2 tbsp. of mushroom pieces in a jar or can, drained

4 beef meatballs, frozen

1/3 cup of beef broth, ready to use

½ cup of marinara sauce

Instructions:

- Put the frozen meatballs in a microwave-friendly mug and zap them in the microwave, which should be turned high, for 1 to 2 minutes
- Cut the warmed meatballs in half with the use of a fork
- Add the mushrooms, marinara sauce, mixed vegetables, and broth.
- Zap in the microwave, which should be turned high, until heated for 1 ½ to 2 minutes
- Stir in pepper and salt to taste
- Freshly chopped parsley, shredded Parmesan cheese or any other type of cheese can be garnished on the stew

- Delight in this filling stew!

Burrito in a Cup

Ingredients:

120 ml or ½ cup of water

50g or ¼ cup of rice

Any mix you want such as chicken, corn, cheese, beans, tomatoes, chopped spinach, lime juice, peppers, etc.

Instructions:

- In a large microwave-friendly mug, mix the rice and water
- Turn microwave on high and zap the mug for 1-1.5 minutes or until water boils
- As soon as water boils, turn off the microwave and let the mug sit for 1 minute
- Turn the microwave at half-power and zap the mug for another 5-6 minutes
- Turn off the microwave but let the mug sit for another 5 minutes in it
- Remove, and use a fork to fluff the rice
- Add your choice of burrito condiments

- Put the mug back to the microwave and zap for another minute
- Dinner's ready!

Appetizing Mexican Mug Dinner

Ingredients:

1 tbsp. of milk

1 egg

Salt and pepper to taste

1 tbsp. of cheese

1 or two tortillas, crushed

2-3 tbsp. of tomato sauce

½ onion, chopped

Sour cream to taste

Chives per preference

Instructions:

- In a large microwave-friendly mug use a fork to beat in the egg
- Beat in the cheese, milk, salt, and pepper
- Top with crushed tortillas, chopped onion, tomato sauce, and sour cream
- Turn the microwave to its highest setting, and then zap the mug for 1 minute
- Garnish with more sour cream, onion, tomato sauce, and tortillas
- Sit down and enjoy your vaguely Mexican dinner!

A Mug of Meatloaf Goodness

Ingredients:

1/8 tsp of black pepper, ground

1 green onion, sliced thinly

1 slice of bread, white and torn into pieces

¼ tsp of salt

½ tsp of Worcestershire sauce

¼ pound of beef, ground

2 tbsp. of milk

Instructions:

- In a small bowl, put the torn bread; add the Worcestershire sauce and milk
- Let it stand for a few minutes to let the liquid seep to the bread
- Add to the bread mixture pepper, salt, ground beef, and green onion
- Mix them thoroughly
- Transfer to a 10-ounce microwave-friendly mug
- Zap in the microwave set in medium-high heat for 4 to 5 ½ minutes or until beef's center is not pink anymore
- Remove the meatloaf and let it cool for 2 minutes
- Top with desired sauce before eating

Avocado and Egg in a Mug

Ingredients:

2 tbsp. of avocado, diced

½ cup of fresh spinach, chopped

1 wedge of Creamy and Light Swiss cheese

½ cup of mushrooms, sliced

2 tbsp. of tomatoes, diced

½ cup of liquid egg substitute, fat-free

1 tbsp. of hot sauce

Instructions:

- Spray a large microwave-friendly mug with non-stick spray and add mushrooms and spinach
- Nuke the mug in the microwave for 1 ½ minutes until they become soft
- Remove and wipe away the moisture before adding in the egg substitute

- Return to the microwave to nuke for another minute
- Break the cheese wedge and mix in the tomato to the mug mixture
- Zap for another minute
- Top with diced avocado

A Mug-Full of Chicken Pie

Ingredients:

For the Chicken mixture:

3-4 tbsp. of chicken, cooked

2 tbsp. of vegetables such as carrots and peas, frozen

1 ½ tsp of cornstarch or cornflour

Salt and pepper to taste

1 tbsp. of cream or milk, full-fat

3 tbsp. of chicken stock

For the topping:

1 tbsp. of herbs, chopped

4 tbsp. of flour

3 ½ tbsp. of buttermilk or milk

½ tsp of baking powder

9g or 1/4oz or ½ tbsp. of cubed butter

1/8 tsp of salt

Instructions:

- Combine the cornstarch, cooked chicken, salt, pepper, and frozen vegetables in a large microwave-friendly mug
- Mix well until cornstarch is dissolved. Set the mixture aside
- In a small bowl, make your topping by combining salt, flour, and baking powder
- Add the cubed butter to the dry ingredients by using a fork until it looks like very fine breadcrumbs
- Add the herbs and milk and mix well until batter becomes smooth
- Use a spoon to scoop the batter to the chicken mixture
- You might notice that the batter will sink a bit, which should not be a cause for worry as it will rise during cooking

- Nuke the mug in the microwave from 2 minutes to 2 minutes and 15 seconds
- You will know that the food is cooked when the batter becomes firm to the touch
- Enjoy this hearty chicken pie cooked in a mug!

Chapter 5 - Quick and easy to make mug meal snacks

Snacks are part and parcel of our lives, especially on busy days when we need to replenish our energy levels. The recipes for mug meal snacks are not only easy to make, but are lifesavers as well.

Blueberry Flax Muffin in a Mug

Ingredients:

½ tsp of nutmeg

¼ cup of flaxseed, ground

½ tsp of zest of an orange

1 ounce of blueberries, frozen

½ tsp of baking powder

1 egg white

2 tbsp. of pancake syrup, sugar-free

Instructions:

- Mix thoroughly all the dry ingredients in a big measuring cup
- Add to the dry mixture the zest of an orange, egg white, and pancake syrup
- Spray a large mug or coffee cup with a bit of cooking oil
- Pour the mixture in the sprayed mug
- Zap in the microwave for 90 seconds
- Be prepared to see a tall muffin

- Using a shallow bowl will give you a flatter muffin
- You can top the cooked muffin with either a little butter or a little more of the pancake syrup
- A sinfully delicious muffin can be yours if you add a tablespoon of melted butter to the muffin mixture before cooking

French toast in a Cup

Ingredients:

One or two slices of bread (any kind)

A pat of butter

1 egg

A pinch of cinnamon

A drop of vanilla (optional) per preference

3 tbsp. of milk

Instructions:

- Rub a pat of butter inside the mug. Another option is to use the microwave to melt the butter inside the mug
- Cut the bread in cubes and put them inside the mug, but not packed tightly
- In another bowl, use a fork to mix the egg, a pinch of cinnamon, milk, and vanilla
- Drizzle the mixture to the mug containing the cubed bread

- Mix them well and allow a minute for the bread to soak it all
- Zap them to the microwave and cook for a minute and 10 seconds
- If you find it a bit runny, zap it again for another 10 seconds
- Top with either syrup or whip cream

A Cup of Chocolate Chip Cookie

Ingredients:

1-2 tbsp. of chocolate chips

1 tbsp. of butter, unsalted

A pinch or 1/8 tsp of salt

3 tbsp. of flour, all-purpose

1 tbsp. of sugar, granulated

½ tsp of vanilla extract

1 egg yolk

1 tbsp. of firmly packed brown sugar

Instructions:

- Melt the butter by putting it in a microwave-friendly mug and zapping it in the microwave from 30 seconds to 1 minute
- Using a spoon, add salt, sugars, and vanilla extract, mixing them well
- Add the egg yolk and mix thoroughly
- Add the flour and chocolate chips

- Zap the mixture in the microwave, which should be turned high, between 40 to 50 seconds
- Top with ice cream or eat while it's still warm

Brownie Mug

Ingredients:

3 tbsp. of chocolate chips with half of semi-sweet and the other half of milk chocolate

2 tbsp. of cocoa powder

2 tbsp. of butter, salted kind

Pinch of salt

¼ cup of brown sugar, lightly packed

¼ cup of flour, all purpose

1 large egg

1 pinch of baking soda

¼ tsp of vanilla extract

Instructions:

- In a large microwave-friendly mug, add brown sugar and butter
- Turn the microwave high and zap for 45 seconds

- Remove from microwave, using a fork to stir the mixture
- Add vanilla extract and egg
- Continue stirring as you add salt, flour, and baking soda
- Stir until batter becomes smooth
- Add the chocolate chips
- Turn microwave to medium heat and cook the brownie for 1 minute and 50 seconds or 2 minutes 30 seconds depending on the wattage of your microwave
- Do not overcook or your brownie will become dry and tough
- Top with caramel sauce, ice cream or chocolate sauce
- Eat while warm and enjoy!

A Mug of Banana Bread

Ingredients:

1 mashed ripe banana

2 tbsp. of brown sugar

Non-stick cooking spray

1 tbsp. of milk

3 tbsp. of flour

¼ tsp of vanilla extract

1 egg

1/8 tsp of baking powder

1 tbsp. and 1 tsp sugar

1/8 tsp of baking soda

1 tbsp. of vegetable oil

Instructions:

- Spray a microwave-friendly mug with non-stick cooking spray
- Combine and mix the baking soda, baking powder, salt, flour, and sugar right in the mug
- Add the egg and stir well until well-blended
- Stir in the mashed banana, vanilla, milk, and oil
- Nuke in the microwave for 3 minutes and check after 90 seconds to see if cake is done

- Remove and let cool
- Enjoy the goodness and healthy benefits of this banana snack!

Chapter 6 - Sinfully decadent mug desserts

Sinfully decadent desserts are great stress relievers we need to indulge in from time to time or all the time! The good news is that those seemingly difficult luscious delights can now be easily and quickly baked in a microwave using a microwave-friendly mug.

So be sinful and try these simple but mouth-watering desserts that come in a mug:

Lusciously Moist Hazelnut and Chocolate Cake in a Mug

I'm pretty sure you're nuts with Nutella just like everyone is these days. If you are another fan of Nutella, this lusciously moist hazelnut and chocolate cake you can bake in a mug will make you look forward to the next serving.

Ingredients:

5 tbsp. of flour, self-rising

5 tbsp. of chocolate hazelnut or Nutella spread, and extra helpings for garnish

½ tsp of vanilla extract

2 tbsp. of vegetable oil

2 tbsp. of milk

2 tbsp. of brown sugar

1 egg

Instructions:

- Melt in two microwave-friendly mugs for about 10 to 15 seconds the Nutella and oil. Stir.
- Stir in the brown sugar and allow the mixture to cool a bit before adding in the egg
- Use a fork to beat in the egg
- Add vanilla and milk
- Stir in the flour and continue stirring until batter becomes smooth
- The batter should only come halfway to the cups, so divide them evenly
- Baking should only be done one cup at a time

- Zap one mug in the microwave for around 60 to 70 seconds
- Once cake has risen, zap it for an additional 10 to 15 seconds
- You can check if cake is cooked by pricking the center with the tines of a fork
- Be careful not to overcook the cake because it will become spongy
- Let the cake cool before topping it with whipped cream, melted Nutella or ice cream
- Cakes are best eaten after they are cooked

Red Velvet Cake in a Mug

Ingredients:

<u>Frosting for the cake</u>

½ cup of sugar

2 tbsp. of cream cheese

2 tbsp. of butter

The cake

½ tsp of food coloring, red

4 tbsp. of flour

3 tbsp. of buttermilk

1 egg

4 ½ tbsp. of sugar

1 ½ tbsp. of cocoa powder, unsweetened

3 tbsp. of oil

1/8 tsp of baking powder

Instructions:

- With the use of a fork, mix all the ingredients in a large microwave-friendly mug
- Stir until batter is smooth
- Zap in the microwave for around 1 minute and 30 seconds
- Zap for another 30 seconds if cake is still uncooked

- Do not overcook as cake may become rubbery and tough

The frosting:

- Mix all the frosting ingredients in a mixing bowl
- Turn speed on high until fluffy and light
- You may either pipe it or spread on top of the cake
- Enjoy the treat!

Yummy Lemon Mug Cake

Ingredients:

For the cake:

1 ½ tbsp. of lemon juice, freshly squeezed

3 tbsp. of flour, all purpose

2 tbsp. of vegetable oil

1/8 tsp of salt

¼ tsp of baking powder

1 tsp of lemon zest, grated finely

3 tbsp. of sugar, granulated

1 egg, large

For the frosting on the cake:

1 ½ lemon juice, freshly squeezed

1/3 cup of icing or confectioner's sugar

Instructions:

For the cake:

- With the use of a fork, mix all the ingredients in a microwave-friendly mug
- Stir thoroughly until batter becomes smooth
- Zap in the microwave from 1 ½ to 2 minutes or until cake has risen with center firm to the touch
- Set aside to cool and prepare the frosting

<u>For the frosting:</u>

- Using a small bowl and fork, mix in lemon juice and confectioner's sugar
- Stir until it becomes smooth
- Pour over the cake
- Marvel at the taste!

Nutella Cake in a Mug

Ingredients:

3 tbsp. of vegetable or olive oil

4 tbsp. of flour

3 tbsp. of cocoa powder

3 tbsp. of milk

4 tbsp. of white sugar, granulated

3 tbsp. of Nutella

1 egg

Instructions:

- In a large microwave-friendly mug, use a fork to mix all the ingredients
- Stir well until batter becomes smooth
- Zap in a microwave, which should be turned high, for 1 ½-3 minutes
- Enjoy more of this sinful delight by topping it with chocolate syrup, your choice of fresh fruit or whipped cream

Moist Chocolate Cake in a Mug

Ingredients:

1-2 tbsp. of cocoa powder or as per your preference

1 egg

¼ cup of powdered sugar

Instructions:

- In a microwave-friendly mug, combine the cocoa powder, egg, and powdered sugar using a small whisk
- Whisk until batter is smooth
- Zap in a microwave for 50-60 seconds or until cake is cooked
- Do not overcook or cake will become tough and rubbery
- Top with your preferred toppings such as whipped cream, ice cream, hot fudge or chocolate chips
- Don't think of your waistline as you indulge in this sinful treat!

Peach Cobbler Cake in a Mug

Ingredients:

1 peaches in light syrup, diced

1-2 pinches of cinnamon

A small pinch of nutmeg

1 tbsp. of butter

2 ½ tbsp. of milk

3 tbsp. of white cake mix

2 tbsp. of liquid from the canned peaches

Instructions:

- In a microwave-friendly mug, put butter and melt it in the microwave
- Get a small bowl and whisk cinnamon, nutmeg, and cake mix together
- Add the milk and whisk until smooth
- Without stirring, pour the batter to the mug
- Add 2 tbsp. of the liquid from the can of peaches
- Top it with peaches without stirring
- Turn microwave on medium-high heat and zap for around 3-4 minutes until cake is cooked
- Remove the mug from the microwave and let it stand for 2-3 minutes or until cool
- Top with ice cream and a sprinkle of cinnamon
- Enjoy the treat!

Cheesecake in a Mug

Ingredients:

2-4 tbsp. of sugar substitute replacement (per preference)

2 oz. of softened cream cheese

¼ tsp of vanilla

2 tbsp. of sour cream

½ tsp lemon juice

1 egg

Instructions:

- In a microwave-friendly mug or bowl, combine all the ingredients until well-blended
- Turn microwave on high heat and zap the mug for 30 seconds
- Stir the mixture well and zap it again for another 30 seconds
- Stir the mixture again and nuke it for the last time for 30 seconds
- For a perfect cheesecake experience, top it with whipped cream or your favorite fresh fruit

Chocolaty and Decadent s'more cake in a mug

Ingredients:

Graham cracker crumbs enough to fill two 12 oz microwave-friendly mugs with extras for topping

Pinch of salt

1 egg yolk

5 tbsp of flour, self-rising

3 tbsp of butter, divided between the two mugs

1 tbsp of cocoa powder

3 tbsp and ¼ cup milk chocolate chips divided between two mugs

10 to 12 mini marshmallows

2 tbsp of sugar

2 tbsp of milk

½ tsp of vanilla extract

Instructions:

- Lightly spray the two mugs with cooking oil before adding ½ tbsp butter to each mug
- Melt the butter by zapping it for a few seconds in the microwave
- Evenly distribute the graham crumbs between the two cups, stir and set aside

- Using another microwave-friendly bowl which can hold 2 cups, spoon in ¼ cup of chocolate chips and 2 tablespoons of butter
- Zap between 20 to 25 seconds in the microwave or until melted
- Remove, stir, and add in sugar. Stir
- Add egg yolks when the mixture has cooled
- Use a fork to beat in the eggs then add in the vanilla extract and milk
- Stir in 3 tablespoons of chocolate chips, flour, salt, and cocoa
- Continue stirring until batter becomes smooth
- Put a tablespoon of batter to each cup
- Top each cup with 5 or 6 mini marshmallows
- Top it with the remaining batter, evenly distributing it between the two cups which should only be filled halfway

- Bake one cup at a time by zapping it between 60 to 70 seconds
- Time 10 to 15 seconds baking time to the cake as soon as it rises and peaks
- Cake may flatten but a springy feel will tell you cake is cooked
- You can give another 10 to 15 seconds baking time if the cake remains uncooked
- An overdone cake will be spongy and tough so do not overcook
- You may add additional toppings like chocolate chips or marshmallows zapping it in the microwave for a few second to melt them
- Another innovative idea to soften toppings would be the use of a broiler or torch
- The remaining graham crumbs can be used to garnish over the cake

- The best time to enjoy eating a cake is right after it's cooked and prepared

Conclusion

The highly urbanized lifestyle of the modern age has ushered a lot of changes in the lives of people like you and me. Condominium living is now the norm rather than the form with furniture and home decors veering more to the minimalist style.

Chunky and heavy furniture are out while sleek, colorful, and space-saving ones are in. Small herbal gardens inside the condominium are in as a way to save on space, yet create a green oasis in the middle of high urbanized living.

Cooking styles and methods have also evolved into something that has to keep up with the busyness of the world. Yet, taste buds remain the same and people still crave for good food that can only be enjoyed at a great price: too much and too long food preparations.

It's not surprising then when people became mad over mug cooking when it hit the scene. Now gourmet cooking can be yours at a cup's notice!

Microwaves have become a necessity rather than a luxury. It was first used as great food warmers for leftover or cold foods. A genius thought of using a cup, a microwave, and voila, cooking in a mug is born.

I hope that the amazing recipes compiled in this book have broadened your cooking horizons, stunning you with its quick and easy preparations.

I hope that this book has made you see that mug cooking is a great way of learning to cook easily, quickly, and deliciously whenever you are too lazy or do not have the luxury of time to do so.

I hope that this book has made you see that yes, you can have your 3 meals and in-between snacks come directly from a mug.

I hope that this book has kindled your interest in cooking and baking when you see how easy it is to cook.

I hope that this book has given you an idea that a microwave and a couple of microwave-friendly mugs and cups can be wonderful kitchen accessories which readily takes away the unappealing effort of washing pans and pots as well as plates.

Thank you for stopping by to give me company while I share all the delightful and delicious mug recipes that I have made and enjoyed. I hope you enjoyed the same culinary delights of these mug recipes just as I did writing them.

CPSIA information can be obtained
at www.ICGtesting.com
Printed in the USA
BVHW041007020520
579069BV00014B/3441

9 781533 324382